PARASITES

Salmonella

Kris Hirschmann

KIDHAVEN
PRESS™

THOMSON

GALE

San Diego • Detroit • New York • San Francisco • Cleveland
New Haven, Conn. • Waterville, Maine • London • Munich

© 2004 by KidHaven Press. KidHaven Press is an imprint of The Gale Group, Inc.,
a division of Thomson Learning, Inc.

KidHaven™ and Thomson Learning™ are trademarks used herein under license.

For more information, contact
KidHaven Press
27500 Drake Rd.
Farmington Hills, MI 48331-3535
Or you can visit our Internet site at http://www.gale.com

LIBRARY OF CONGRESS CATALOGING-IN-PUBLICATION DATA

Hirschmann, Kris
    Salmonella / by Gail Jarrow.
      v. cm. — (Parasites)
Includes bibliographical references (p.   ) and index.
Contents: Human-loving parasites—bacteria—The fight against salmonella
    ISBN 0-7377-1785-8 (hardback : alk. paper)
    1. Salmonella—Juvenile literature. 2. Bacteria Salmonella—Juvenile literature.
[1] Salmonella.] I. Title. II. Series.
    RA641.S6H55 2004
    615.4'9'63—dc22
                                                                    2003009614

Printed in the United States

C O N T E N T S

Bacterial Parasites

Several hours after eating a meal, a man starts to feel queasy and dizzy. His stomach hurts, he has diarrhea, and he starts to vomit. What is wrong with this man? There is a good chance he has been infected by salmonella.

Salmonella are **parasites**, which means they live inside and feed on animals. These animals are called **hosts**.

Why Parasites?

Salmonella are a type of **bacteria**. Bacteria are one-celled **microorganisms** that live everywhere on Earth. Many types of bacteria live comfortably in soil, water, and other nonliving matter. However, some types of bacteria—including salmonella—reproduce inside animals. Bacteria that need living hosts are considered parasites.

Salmonella are bacteria that reproduce inside people and animals.

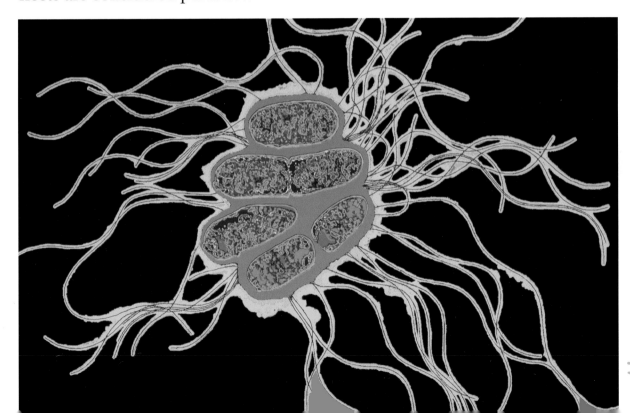

Salmonella Basics

More than two thousand different types of salmonella bacteria exist. In the United States, the most common varieties are **Salmonella enteritidis** and **typhimurium**. Both of these varieties cause an illness called **salmonellosis**, which is an intestinal disorder. The disorder is also called **salmonella gastroenteritis**. About forty thousand cases of this illness are reported each year in the United States. However, most people who get salmonellosis do not go to a doctor. So the actual number of cases is probably much higher—perhaps as high as 2 million per year.

In other parts of the world, **Salmonella typhi** is common. This strain of salmonella causes a serious disease called **typhoid fever**. Typhoid fever spreads easily in **unsanitary** conditions, and it kills up to 20 percent of its victims.

Getting Around

Most salmonella infections begin when a person eats contaminated food. Eggs and raw meats are the

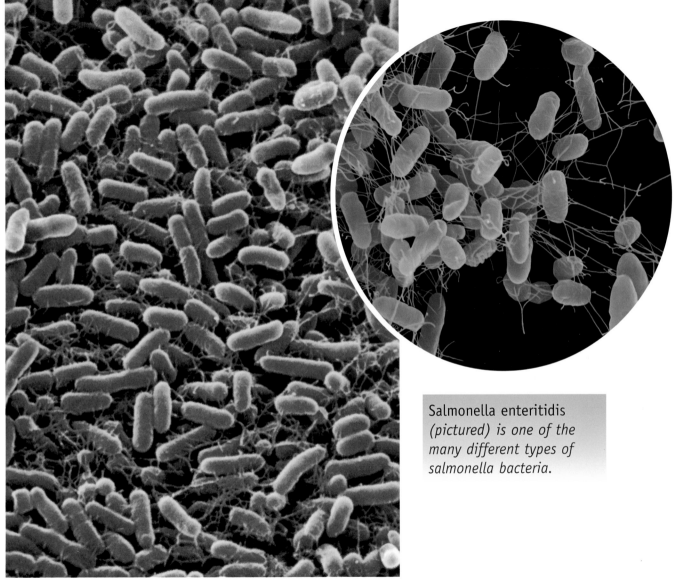

Salmonella enteritidis *(pictured) is one of the many different types of salmonella bacteria.*

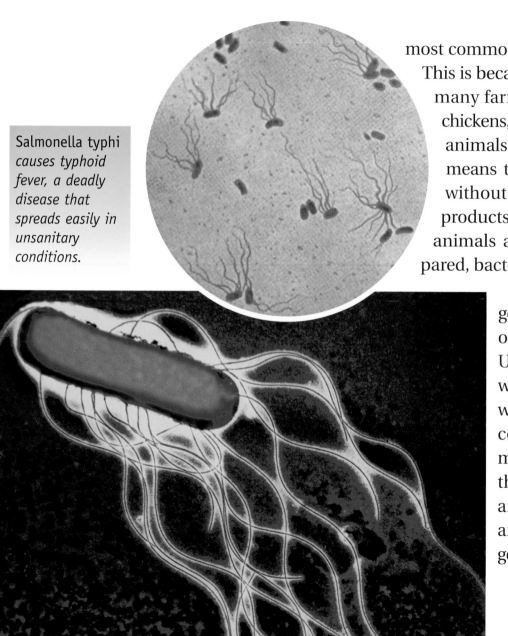

Salmonella typhi *causes typhoid fever, a deadly disease that spreads easily in unsanitary conditions.*

most common sources of infection. This is because salmonella live in many farm animals, including chickens, pigs, and cows. These animals are **carriers**, which means they host the bacteria without getting sick. If food products that come from these animals are not properly prepared, bacteria can remain.

Salmonella can also get onto vegetables and other nonanimal foods. Usually this happens when the foods are washed in water that contains traces of animal droppings. Even though the foods look and smell clean, they are crawling with dangerous bacteria.

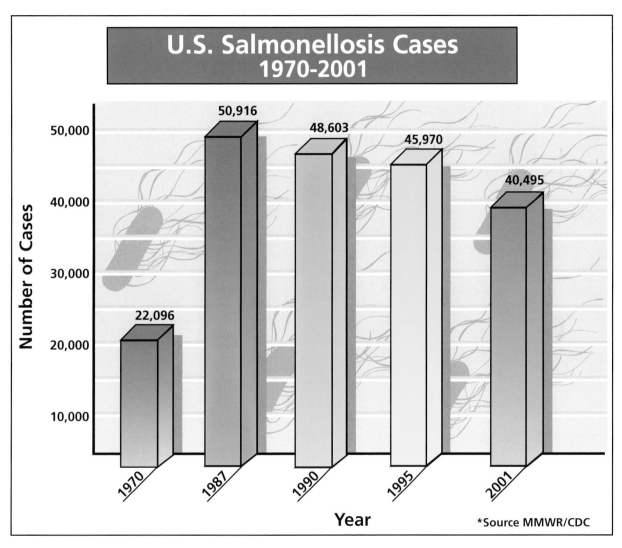

U.S. Salmonellosis Cases 1970-2001

Number of Cases

- 1970: 22,096
- 1987: 50,916
- 1990: 48,603
- 1995: 45,970
- 2001: 40,495

Year

*Source MMWR/CDC

Occasionally people get sick after they touch salmonella-infested animals. Bacteria get onto their hands. Then the people put their dirty hands into their mouths.

A Common Problem

Salmonella bacteria do not hide only in food. They also lurk in kitchen sinks, on cutting boards, on countertops, and anywhere else food is prepared or stored. Even a dirty knife or plate can spread disease.

Because salmonella are so common, they are hard to avoid. People eat salmonella bacteria all the time, and they often become sick as a result. Over a lifetime, almost everyone will become the victim of these tiny parasites.

CHAPTER 2

The Parasite Strikes

Salmonella enter the body through the mouth. They move down the throat and into the stomach along with any food a person has eaten.

In the stomach, strong acids dissolve a person's meal. Most of the time they also kill salmonella bacteria. But sometimes a few bacteria survive the acid bath. They pass alive into the small intestine, where they launch an attack on their human host.

The Course of Infection

As soon as salmonella enter the intestine, they start swimming. They do this by waving tiny, whiplike hairs called **flagella**. Soon the bacteria reach the intestinal wall, where they begin to split themselves in two. The bacteria colony grows quickly. Before long, millions of these microorganisms are wriggling through the host's intestines.

As the salmonella split, they enter and kill the cells of the intestinal wall. They also create **toxins**, substances that are poisonous to human tissue. Both of these processes irritate the intestines. In response, white blood cells (the human body's main defense against harm-

Salmonella enter the intestine (left) and kill the cells of the intestinal wall (above).

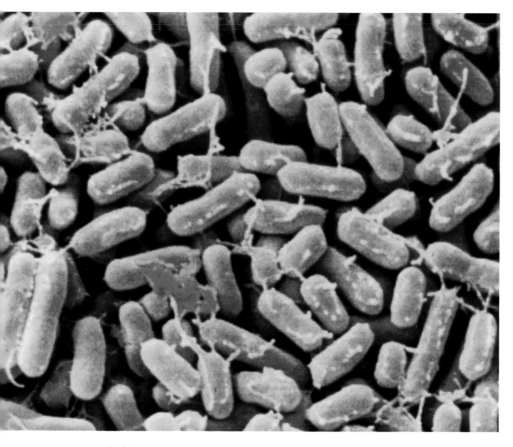

ful bacteria and viruses) rush to the site of infection. They attack and kill the salmonella bacteria. They will continue attacking until all of the invaders are dead.

Symptoms of Infection

Salmonellosis usually strikes between six and forty-eight hours after a person eats infected food. The first symptoms are stomachache, severe nausea, and vomiting. Fever, intestinal cramps, and diarrhea soon follow. Sometimes the diarrhea contains blood that has seeped from the damaged intestinal walls.

These symptoms are signs of the battle raging within. Nausea and vomiting eject bacteria from the stomach. Diarrhea occurs because the intestine starts oozing liquids to soothe damaged tissue. And fever weakens the invaders. Salmonella reproduce best at normal human body temperature, so fever is the body's way of slowing this process.

Salmonellosis does not usually last long. Most infections disappear within a week. But occasionally a salmonella infection gets bad enough to kill its host. In the United States, between five hundred and a thousand people die each year from salmonella poisoning.

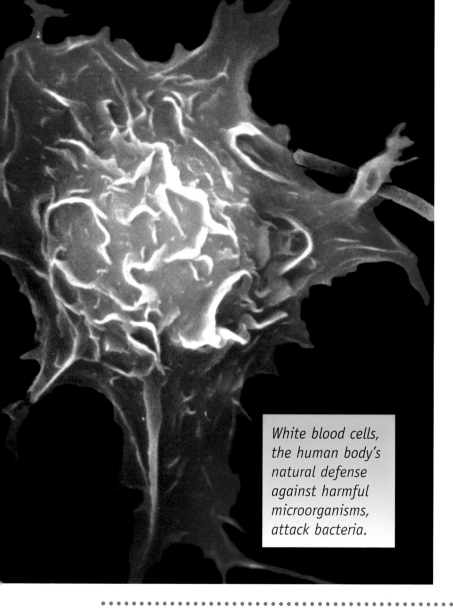

White blood cells, the human body's natural defense against harmful microorganisms, attack bacteria.

Complications

Most salmonella infections stay in the intestine. Sometimes, however, the bacteria pass through the intestinal wall and into the bloodstream. They travel to the host's liver, spleen, heart, and other organs, where they settle and begin reproducing again.

A salmonella infection that spreads through the system is called **enteric fever**. Enteric fevers (including typhoid fever) often start as regular bouts of gastroenteritis. After a few days the symptoms disappear. But about a week later, a new wave of illness hits. The victim's temperature rises to 103 or 104 degrees Fahrenheit. He or she also feels weak and has stomach pains, severe headaches, and sometimes a skin

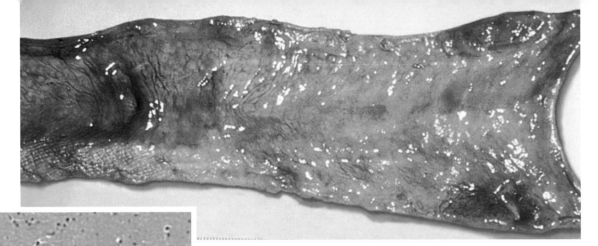

Salmonella bacteria spread throughout the body through the bloodstream. Here, Salmonella typhi *have infected the gall bladder (above) and brain tissue (left).*

rash. If the infection is not treated, it may last for months. The host may even die.

Even after a salmonella infection is gone, problems may remain. Some victims develop joint pain, eye trouble, and other symptoms that can last for years. These symptoms are reminders of a tiny—but powerful—parasite.

CHAPTER 3

Salmonella Stories

The worst salmonellosis outbreak in U.S. history occurred between late March and early April 1985. Patients with nausea, vomiting, diarrhea, and other symptoms of salmonella poisoning jammed doctors' offices in the Chicago area. By the time the episode ended, more than sixteen thousand people had been treated.

Investigators eventually discovered the cause of this outbreak. A local dairy had accidentally sold

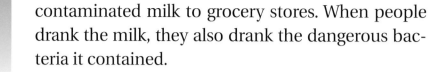

contaminated milk to grocery stores. When people drank the milk, they also drank the dangerous bacteria it contained.

Poisoned Food

Although salmonella can lurk in store-bought foods, as in the Chicago incident, most cases start in people's homes. Undercooked food is the major cause of salmonellosis.

A typical case occurred in Nevada in 1995. Seven people gathered for a Thanksgiving dinner of turkey

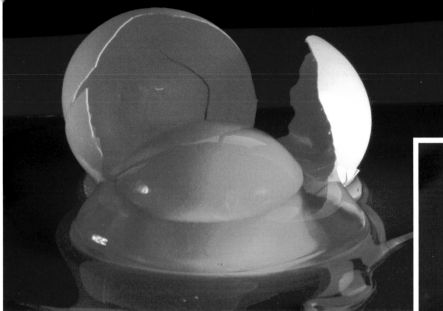

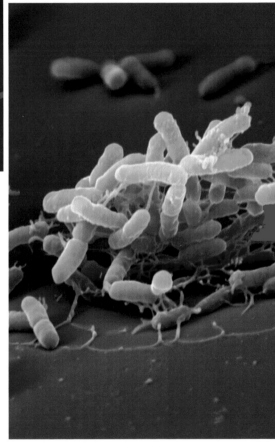

and stuffing. The food tasted delicious. But two days after the Thanksgiving feast, all seven people became ill. Three of the people were so sick that they had to be hospitalized, and one of these people eventually died.

The local health department investigated the incident. They discovered that the stuffing these people had eaten contained raw eggs, the most common source of salmonella poisoning. The stuffing had been cooked, but not long enough to kill the bacteria. Each tasty bite was crawling with disease.

Dangerous Pets

Pet reptiles can also cause salmonellosis. Snakes, turtles, lizards, and other reptiles are carriers, and they can spread bacteria to their owners.

One family learned this lesson when their six-week-old infant became ill with diarrhea, fever, and a stiff neck. Doctors discovered that the family had a pet turtle. The baby never touched the turtle, but other family members did. Someone in the family had gotten the turtle's bacteria on his or her hands, then touched and infected the baby.

Because the baby was so young, his illness was very serious. He eventually recovered, but he had to stay in the hospital for nearly two months before he was well enough to go home.

Typhoid Fever

Another serious salmonella incident occurred in Maryland in 1994. A pregnant woman came to the hospital complaining of fever and chills. She was also having early labor contractions. Doctors feared the woman was going to lose her baby.

A young girl carefully handles a python. Pet reptiles can spread salmonella to their owners.

It turned out that the woman had just returned from a trip to India, where typhoid fever is common. Tests confirmed that the woman had the disease. Drug treatment cured the woman and saved her baby, but the process required more than two months of hospitalization.

Typhoid Mary

Some people who catch typhoid fever recover but continue to carry the bacteria in their bodies. These carriers can infect others if they prepare food.

History's best-known typhoid carrier was named Mary Mallon. Mallon worked as a cook in New York in the early 1900s. She passed typhoid fever to at least fifty-three people; five of these people died. "Typhoid Mary," as she was called, was eventually caught by local health officials and forced to live alone for the rest of her life so she could not infect anyone else.

A typhoid carrier would not be treated like this today. Instead of being locked away, a carrier would receive drugs to kill the salmonella bacteria in his or her body. Thanks to modern medicine, these parasites are much less frightening than they were a hundred years ago.

Controlling the Parasite

N o one knew exactly what caused salmonellosis until 1885, when an American scientist named Daniel Salmon isolated and identified some salmonella bacteria. (The microorganisms were named after their discoverer.) Later research by other scientists uncovered many different strains of salmonella. It soon became clear that these parasites were incredibly common.

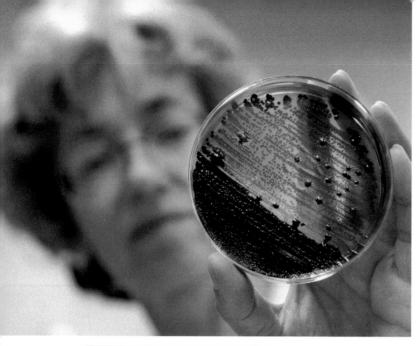

A scientist studies salmonella bacteria in a laboratory.

By the 1940s, people knew that salmonella bacteria were a major cause of food poisoning. They were starting to learn what types of foods and animals carried salmonella, and they were also learning how to stop the parasite from spreading.

Food Safety

Since 95 percent of all salmonellosis infections come from food, careful food preparation is the best way to stay safe. Refrigeration is the first step. Salmonella cannot reproduce at low temperatures, so cold or frozen food is much safer than warm or room-temperature food.

Thorough cooking is the next step. Heat kills salmonella bacteria, so meat, eggs, and other foods that tend to carry these parasites must be cooked all the way through. If any raw spots remain, people can get sick.

It is also important to wash anything that has touched salmonella-prone foods. Bacteria can live on cutting boards, plates, knives, and countertops that are not cleaned well. They can also get onto people's skin. People who prepare food must wash their hands with soap and water after handling raw meats and eggs. And anyone who has a salmonella infection should not give food to others until the infection is gone.

Salmonella colonies as seen through a microscope. Understanding how salmonella spreads is an important part of stopping the harmful bacteria.

Stopped at the Source

Many salmonella bacteria can be stopped at the source: farming and food processing operations. The U.S. government has strict rules for these businesses. For instance, farmers must inspect

Baby chickens are showered with a special salmonella-killing spray.

their animals often and remove any that carry salmonella. Machinery in food processing operations must be clean and germ-free at all times.

Even the cleanest conditions, however, cannot stop all salmonella bacteria. Therefore, many foods are treated before they are sent to the market. Eggs and meat products are exposed to radiation that kills salmonella. Dairy products are **pasteurized**, which means they are heated to destroy any bacteria they contain.

In recent years, some farmers have been experimenting with sprays that kill salmonella in chickens. Others are testing livestock **vaccines**—substances that make animals immune to salmonella infection. By keeping their animals salmonella-free, farmers hope to keep their food clean, too.

Human Vaccination

There is a human vaccine for typhoid fever. There is no vaccine, however, that protects people against nontyphoid salmonellosis. Careful food handling is the only way to avoid this illness.

Unfortunately, it is very easy to make mistakes in the kitchen. One unwiped countertop or dirty cutting board can spread disease. So can food that sits out just a little too long, or food that needs a few more minutes in the oven. Most people accidentally serve or eat unsafe food during their lifetimes—and most eventually pay the price. Nearly everyone gets salmonellosis at some point. Today, as in ages past, this parasite is an unpleasant fact of human life.

bacteria: One-celled organisms that live everywhere on Earth.

carrier: A person or animal that carries bacteria without becoming sick from them.

enteric fever: A disease caused when salmonella spread throughout the host's system.

flagella (fluh-JELL-uh): Whiplike hairs on the outside of a bacterium.

host: A plant or animal whose body provides shelter and/or food for a parasite.

microorganism: Any organism that is too small to be seen without a microscope.

parasite: An organism that lives in or feeds from another living organism.

pasteurized: Heated to kill bacteria.

Salmonella enteritidis **(en-terr-IT-id-uss):** One strain of salmonella bacteria. It is a common cause of salmonellosis.

salmonella gastroenteritis (GAS-troh-en-terr-ITE-uss): A disorder caused when salmonella reproduce inside the host's intestines.

Salmonella typhi (TYE-fee): One strain of salmonella bacteria. It causes typhoid fever.

Salmonella typhimurium (tye-fih-MYUR-ee-um): One strain of salmonella bacteria. It is a common cause of salmonellosis.

salmonellosis (SAL-mun-ell-OH-sis): Any salmonella infection.

toxins: Substances that are poisonous to human tissue.

typhoid fever: An enteric fever caused by the *Salmonella typhi* strain of salmonella.

unsanitary: Not clean.

vaccine: A substance that, when taken into the body, causes immunity to a disease.

Books

Anne Capeci, *The Giant Germ*. New York: Scholastic, 2000. In this book, Ms. Frizzle and the Magic School Bus kids explore the world of germs.

Howard Facklam and Margery Facklam, *Parasites*. New York: Twenty-First Century Books, 1994. Read about bloodsucking parasites, invasive worms, harmful bacteria, and more in this book.

Kurt Ray, *Typhoid Fever*. New York: Rosen, 2002. This book tells the stories of Typhoid Mary and some typhoid outbreaks. It also discusses the search for the disease's cause and cure.

Linda Wasmer Smith, *Louis Pasteur: Disease Fighter*. Springfield, NJ: Enslow, 1997. A biography of Louis Pasteur, the "father of microbiology" and the inventor of pasteurization.

Website

Bad Bug Book (www.ncagr.com). A kid-friendly explanation of many dangerous food-borne bacteria, including salmonella.

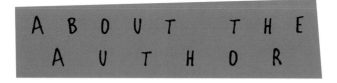

ABOUT THE AUTHOR

Kris Hirschmann has written more than eighty books for children. She is the president of The Wordshop, a business that provides a variety of writing and editorial services. She holds a bachelor's degree in psychology from Dartmouth College in Hanover, New Hampshire. Hirschmann lives just outside Orlando, Florida, with her husband, Michael, and her daughter, Nikki.